GO FOR THE GOAL

Written by Matthew Damman
Illustration by Patty Eisenbraun

Published by MAP Creative LLC

Created and printed in the USA.
Signature Book Printing, www.sbpbooks.com

For information contact MAP Creative LLC at:
info@thesmallsports.com
Visit us at:

www.thesmallsports.com
www.facebook.com/thesmallsports

First Edition

Library of Congress Cataloging-in-Publication Data
Control Number: 2014905357
Damman, Matthew
The Small Sports Go for the Goal / Story by Matthew Damman
Illustrations by Patty Eisenbraun

Summary: Claire desperately tries to score a goal in her last soccer game of the season but ends up discovering what it truly means to be a good sport.

ISBN: 978-0-9856967-2-6

To Mom and Dad
- MD

Special Thanks:
Monica Sakala, Leslie Kimball, Julie Foudy, Vanessa Birch,
Jahmal Dokes, Jerome Bettis, Derrick Walker, Cynthia Sirard,
Bill & Debbie Damman, Shauna Damman.

Claire burst into Jake's bedroom, squeezing her soccer ball. It was a sunny spring afternoon, and she couldn't wait to get to Dodgeball Park.

"It's my last game today, Jake!" she said to her little brother.

"I have to score a goal. Hurry, we can't be late!"

Jake grabbed his football and his lucky red wristband. "I'm ready," he said. "Let's rock and roll!"

Sports
TIGERS
GO FALCONS

As they left the house, Claire stopped in the garage.

“Mom,” she sighed, “I haven’t scored a goal all season.”

“Honey, do your best and have fun like you always do,” her mom replied.

But all Claire could think about was scoring a goal.

On the way to the game, Claire and Jake spotted their friend Joey.

Joey might have been a small boy, but he was always full of big ideas.

"What's in your Wonder Wagon today?" Claire asked him.

"Juice boxes, animal crackers and my baseball mitt!" Joey announced. "I've got everything we need for the game."

"Score!" Jake said. "Let's go!"

17
Sports

As they neared the park, Claire grew as quiet as a mouse. Jake knew that she was nervous, so he handed her his lucky red wristband.

"Maybe this will help," he whispered. "And Mom said we can have ice cream after the game too."

"Thanks, little bro." Claire smiled, but the nervous butterflies still swirled in her belly.

At Dodgeball Park, Jake quickly found his friend Noah. Noah loved basketball and big math problems. His lively little puppy, Buddy, went everywhere with him.

"We need to cheer super loud for Claire today," Jake told his pals.

"Count us in!" Noah said. He was always happy to help his friends.

Out on the field, Claire did jumping jacks with her team.

As she hopped and bopped, she said to herself, *"I can do it. I know I can score."*

Claire couldn't wait for the game to start.

When the whistle blew for kickoff,
Claire ran like lightning.

She dashed and dribbled.

She passed and kicked.

She did all she could to score
a goal and help her team win.

19

In the bleachers, Joey handed out snacks while Jake and Noah jumped and shouted, "Go, Claire, go!"

Katie, the youngest Small Sport, showed up waving her pom-poms. She loved to cheer.

Buddy found a pom-pom and shook it too!

The Small Sports rooted for Claire with all their might.

12
10
17

But the minutes ticked away, and the end of the season was near.
Then, Claire's coach called to her, "You're coming out next!"
Claire's heart sank, and tears began to trickle down her cheeks.
She hadn't scored a goal. *What will everyone think?* she worried.

After the game, Claire wanted to hide.

"Great game, honey!" her dad said, giving her a hug.

"But Dad, I didn't score a goal," she sniffled.

"Playing well isn't just about scoring goals. I'm so proud of you," he replied. "Now you should go shake hands with the other team."

"Please, can't we just leave?" Claire begged.

Then, Claire glanced over at her friends. She remembered what they always said when they played: "The Small Sports are good sports!"

And Claire knew what she had to do.

"Dad, I'll be right back."

Claire hurried to hop in line.

"Nice game!" she said to the other team.

"Great season!" she said to her teammates.

Looking around, Claire realized how many new friends she had made on the team.

Making new friends sure is fun! she thought.

At the end of the line, Claire saw her coach.

"Super job this year, Miss Claire!" he said. "You were unselfish and a real team player." And he handed her a bright blue sticker that said Great Teammate on it.

"Thanks so much, Coach," she said. "I tried my best."

Claire proudly put the sticker on her jersey for everyone to see.

Just then, Jake popped up. "Claire, it's ice cream time!"

"Race you there," Claire giggled. "I get rainbow sprinkles!"

"Wait for us!" Noah, Joey and Katie called out.

Buddy couldn't wait for his favorite chewy treat too.

2
GREAT
TEAMMATE
17

CLOSED
GREAT
17
8

At the ice cream parlor, Claire spotted two girls from the other team.

"Nice game today," she said to them. "You guys were really good."

"We remember you," the girls replied. "You were so fast!"

"Thanks!" Claire smiled.

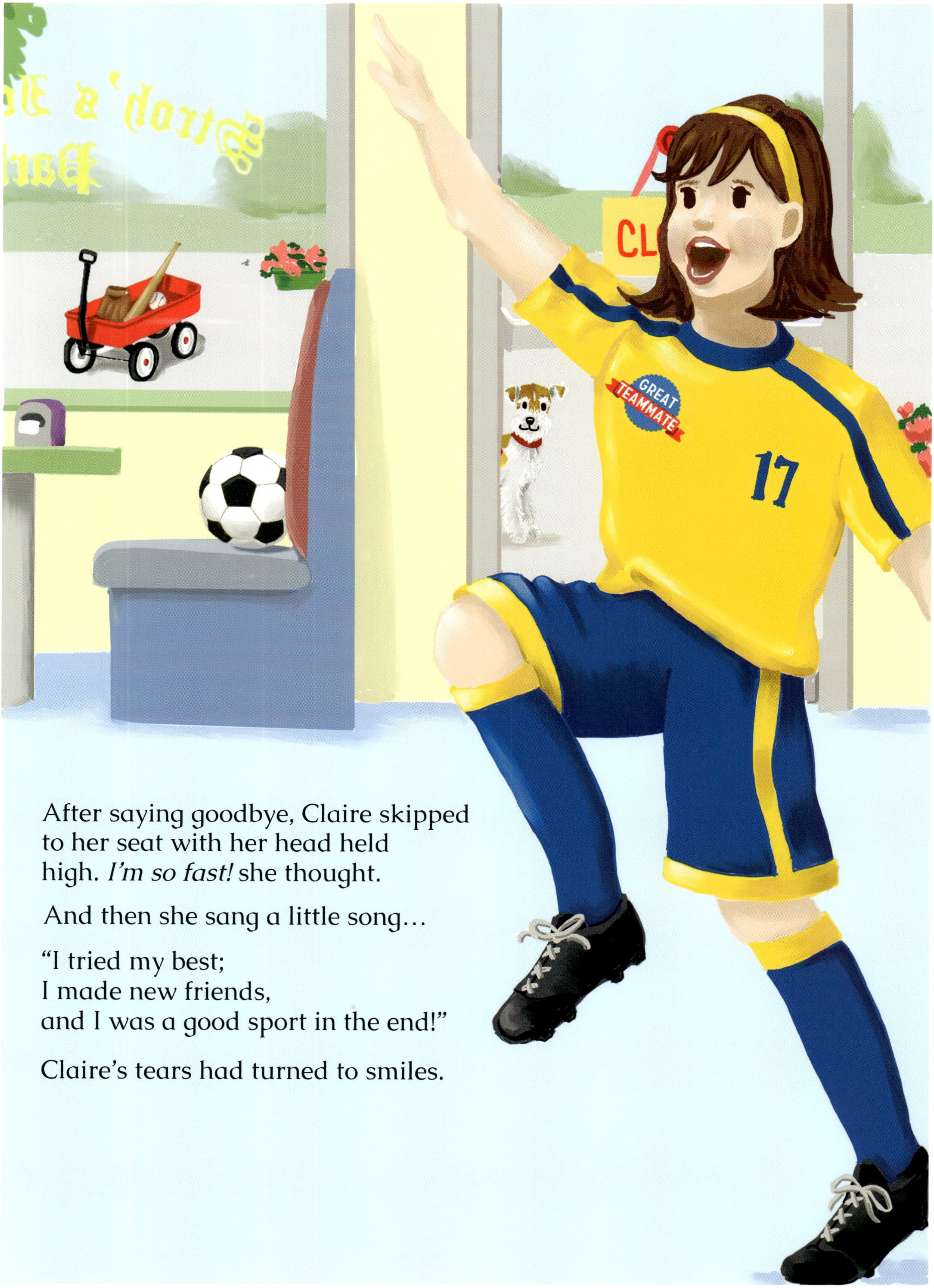

After saying goodbye, Claire skipped to her seat with her head held high. *I'm so fast!* she thought.

And then she sang a little song…

"I tried my best;
I made new friends,
and I was a good sport in the end!"

Claire's tears had turned to smiles.

Back at the table, everyone dug into their tasty treats.

“Sorry the wristband didn’t work,” Jake apologized.

“It’s okay,” Claire said with a smile on her face and her spoon full of sprinkles. “I’m not worried about scoring anymore.”

Claire knew that she was a good sport. And that’s what mattered most.

The Small Sports®

Jake
Jersey #2
Throws right handed

Hi, I'm Jake and I'm 7 years old. I like to play hard and get dirty. My very favorite thing is being at Dodgeball Park with my friends, The Small Sports. Sometimes we lie in the grass and look up at the clouds, and I dream about being a big football player. The things I don't like are loud noises and scary movies. This year, I want to beat my sister, Claire, in a race. She always wins, but I keep trying.

Favorite sayings: "Touchdown!" "That's right!" and "Rock and roll"
Favorite foods: Mac 'n cheese and waffles

Claire
Jersey #17
Height 4' 2"

Hi, I'm Claire, and I'm 8 years old, and I love to run fast. Soccer is my favorite sport, but I like to play everything, even football and kickball. I also like to ride my bike around the block and catch fireflies with my friends. I am nice to everyone I meet because that's what The Small Sports do, and I'm always happy to make new friends. Will you be my friend? I don't like spiders or bugs, but I sure do love chocolate milk!

Favorite dinner: Tacos
Favorite day: Saturday

Buddy
Age – 2

Buddy is Noah's puppy and the official mascot of The Small Sports. He is lively and loyal and loves all sports. He tries his best to shoot baskets and play catch with his toy ball. He loves to cheer the Small Sports on! Woof!

Favorite things: Long walks and chewy treats

www.thesmallsports.com

The SMALL SPORTS®

Noah
Jersey #4
Shoots left handed

Hi there, I'm Noah, and I'm 8 years old. I love to shoot baskets and dribble my basketball. I'm learning to dribble the ball between my legs. Can you dribble between your legs? I also love school, especially math. When I practice, I can add up the number of baskets I shoot in a snap! I take my puppy, Buddy everywhere I go. I even tried to take him to the dentist once!

Favorite saying: "Score!"
Favorite song: We Are the Champions

Joey
Jersey #9
Bats right handed

I'm Joey, and I just turned 7. How old are you? I love baseball. I like to throw, catch and hit. This year, I learned to hit without a tee, and I can almost throw the ball across the whole field. I have a red wagon that is always full of fun stuff like bouncy balls and animal crackers; I even have a baseball that glows in the dark! The Small Sports are my best friends. I hope you can come play with us! Can I tell you a secret? I'm scared of bumblebees!

Favorite food: Pizza
Favorite ice cream: Superman in a cone

Katie

Hi, I'm Katie, and I'm 6 years old. I'm the youngest Small Sport, but my friends are so nice to me. I am a cheerleader and love making up new cheers. Do you cheer for your teammates? I just got new pom-poms and leaned how to do cartwheels, so I'm ready for the next big game. I also love to sing and dance and make my friends smile. I don't like monsters or worms!

Favorite snacks: Popcorn and granola bars
Favorite saying: "You can do it!"

www.thesmallsports.com

Matthew Damman is an author, entrepreneur and co-creator of The Small Sports®. He worked for three Fortune 500 companies before hanging up his suit and tie in 2012 to co-found MAP Creative LLC. Matt graduated from the University of Michigan in 1998. He currently lives in Michigan with his wife Shauna and their two children, Claire and Jake.

Patty Eisenbraun is a professional artist and co-creator of The Small Sports. Art has been her lifelong passion from oil painting to cartoons, to apparel and design. A piece of her work is permanently part of the Smithsonian Institute collection. Patty was also named as one of the top 50 Women in Business by Crain's Detroit and is a board member of the Birmingham-Bloomfield Art Center. She lives in Michigan with her husband Ken, their dogs Buddy and Lucy and Bob, the cat.